Great Quotes for Great Educators

Todd Whitaker
Dale Lumpa

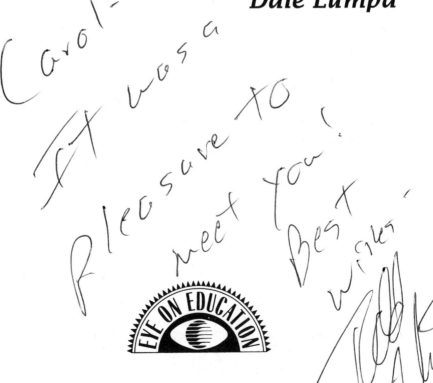

EYE ON EDUCATION

EYE ON EDUCATION
6 DEPOT WAY WEST, SUITE 106
LARCHMONT, NY 10538
(914) 833-0551
(914) 833-0761 fax
www.eyeoneducation.com

Library of Congress Cataloging-in-Publication Data

Great quotes for great educators / Todd Whitaker and Dale Lumpa.
   p. cm.
ISBN 1-930556-82-9
1. Education--Quotations, maxims, etc. I. Whitaker, Todd, 1959- II. Lumpa, Dale, 1961-
PN6084.E38G74 2004
370--dc22

                              2004050623

10 9 8 7 6 5 4 3 2

Editorial and production services provided by
Richard H. Adin, Freelance Editorial Services
52 Oakwood Blvd., Poughkeepsie, NY 12603-4112
(914-471-3566)

Meet the Authors

Dr. Todd Whitaker is a Professor of Educational Leadership at Indiana State University in Terre Haute, Indiana. Prior to coming to Indiana in 1993, he taught at the middle and high school levels in Missouri. Following his teaching experience, he served as a middle school and high school principal for eight years. Dr. Whitaker also served as a middle school coordinator in Jefferson City, Missouri.

Dr. Whitaker's work has been published in the areas of teacher leadership, instructional improvement, change, leadership effectiveness, technology, and middle level practices. His books include *Dealing With Difficult Teachers, Motivating & Inspiring Teachers, Dealing With Difficult Parents, Feeling Great!, Teaching Matters,* and *What Great Principals Do Differently.* His latest book is the number one best seller, What Great Teachers Do Differently. Dr. Whitaker is internationally recognized as an inspirational and distinguished speaker.

Dr. Dale Lumpa is a teacher at Charles Hay Elementary School in Englewood Colorado. He has been an administrator and teacher at the elementary and middle levels for 20 years in Missouri and Colorado.

Dr. Lumpa has presented at state and national conferences on effective discipline, classroom management, and positive strategies for principals and teachers. He has also taught classes focusing on effective leadership and teaching strategies at the University of Phoenix , Indiana State University, and the University of Denver. He has been published in the area of leadership effectiveness and is the coauthor of the book *Motivating and Inspiring Teachers.*

Preface

Great Quotes for Great Educators was a pleasure for us to develop, and we hope it will be a valuable resource for you. As teachers, we loved to scatter inspirational quotes around our classrooms. We would use these quotes on posters that we hoped would help shape the belief systems of our students, or we wrote a quote of the day on the board to enlighten or inspire our young learners. When we became principals, our favorite gems would find their way into our staff memos and parent newsletters. We hoped that by using the words of others we might expand our ability to influence and craft the climate and culture we desired in our schools. We hope you can use some of these quotes for your own purposes.

We wanted to make our book special by adding quotes from real students that share their reflections on teachers, principals, school, and life. These student "echoes" are reminders of what school is actually about. At the end of each chapter, some of these insights are shared so that we can remember our impact as educators.

When writing this book, we learned a very valuable lesson. Though we love to share quotes to influence others, upon reflection, we quite often used these quotes to influence ourselves. We hope you enjoy the book, and we want to thank you for choosing education.

Todd and Dale

Table of Contents

1

The Most Important Profession

Great teachers are made one student at a time.

—*Todd Whitaker*

1

Those who love the young best stay young longest.

—Edgar Friedenberg

My heart is singing for joy this morning. A miracle has happened! The light of understanding has shone upon my little pupil's mind, and, behold, all things are changed.

—Anne Sullivan

Those who can, teach; those who can't, go into some other much less significant line of work.

—Todd Whitaker

In teaching you cannot see the fruit of a day's work. It is invisible and remains so, maybe for twenty years.

—Jacques Barzun

Teaching is the essential profession, the one that makes all professions possible.

—David Haselkorn

We make a living by what we get. We make a life by what we give.

—Winston Churchill

You must learn, you can learn, you will learn. The fact that you have not yet learned means that I have not yet found the way to explain the subject so simply, so clearly, and so exactly that it is impossible for you not to understand. But I will find the way. I will not quit on you.

—Author unknown

Teaching matters.

—Todd Whitaker

To the world you might be just one person; but to just one person, you might be the world.

—Author unknown

A teacher affects eternity; he can never tell where his influence stops.

—Henry Brooke Adams

The greatest use of a life is to spend it for something that will outlast it.

—William James

I touch the future, I teach.

—Christa McAuliffe

There is a giant asleep within every man. When the giant awakes, miracles happen.

—*Frederick Faust*

A good teacher has a love of teaching. A great teacher has a love of learning.

—*Todd Whitaker*

At the desk where I sit, I have learned one great truth. The answer for all our national problems—the answer for all the problems of the world—comes to a single word. That word is education.

—*Lyndon B. Johnson*

I shall be telling this with a sigh
Somewhere ages and ages hence:
Two roads diverged in a wood, and I—
I took the one less traveled by,
And that has made all the difference.

—Robert Frost

I know of no great man except those who have rendered great services to the human race.

—Voltaire

The best and most beautiful things in the world cannot be seen or even touched. They must be felt within the heart.

—Helen Keller

This may be my 28th year teaching 6th grade, but it is the only year that my students are in 6th grade. I have to make it the best year yet!

—Jean Rackers

Good teaching is a good deed.

—Author unknown

Teaching should be such that what is offered is perceived as a valuable gift and not as a hard duty.

—Albert Einstein

What we have done for ourselves alone dies with us; what we have done for others and the world remains and is immortal.

—Albert Pike

It is one of the most beautiful compensations of this life, that no man can sincerely try to help another without helping himself.

—Ralph Waldo Emerson

If you think education is expensive, try ignorance.

—Derek Bok

I don't know what your destiny will be, but one thing I do know: the only ones among you who will be really happy are those who have sought and found how to serve.

—Albert Schweitzer

Service is the rent we pay for living. It is the very purpose of life and not something you do in your spare time.

—Marian Wright Edelman

When teachers reflect on their careers, they will be proudest of the moments when they taught with love.

—Todd Whitaker

Teachers, who educate children, deserve more honor than parents, who merely gave them birth; for the latter provided mere life, while the former ensure a good life.

—Aristotle

Teaching is not a lost art, but the regard for it is a lost tradition.

—Jacques Barzun

I don't think great teachers make a difference. I know it.

—Todd Whitaker

The intelligent have a right over the ignorant; namely, the right of instructing them.

—Ralph Waldo Emerson

Teacher: the child's third parent.

—Hyman Berston

Don't use your students to build a great teaching career; use your teaching career to build great students.

—Todd Whitaker

I have somewhere met with the epitaph of a charitable man which has pleased me very much. I cannot recollect the words, but here is the sense of it: "What I spent I lost; what I possessed is left to others; what I gave away remains with me."

—Joseph Addison

What greater or better gift can we offer the republic than to teach and instruct our youth.

—Cicero

Success in any profession starts with a focus on self. After all, we are the one variable that we can most easily and most productively influence.

—Todd Whitaker

Echoes

Real Quotes from Real Students

- *I really want to be a teacher because you can really make a difference and still be cool.*

- *My favorite things about school are the teachers, boys, and the other teachers.*

- *I want to be a theater teacher for high school students. That way I can inspire those who need inspirations.*

- *Yes, being a teacher changes lives! No other people have such an impact on my life as my teachers do.*

Great Teaching Makes Great Students

2

The excellent teachers did not choose education because of June, July, and August. They chose education because of Julie, Juan, and Amber.

—Todd Whitaker

Great teachers have high expectations for their students, but higher expectations for themselves.

—Todd Whitaker

Your classroom must honor student questions as much as student answers.

—Author unknown

A pro is someone who can do great work when he doesn't feel like it.

—Alistair Cooke

If all learning is zero to ten, then the most important part of learning is zero to one.

—Monty Roberts

Experience isn't the best teacher. The best teacher is the best teacher.

— *Todd Whitaker*

Instead of the sage on the stage, you need to be the guide by the side.

— *Author unknown*

We can, whenever and wherever we choose, successfully teach all children whose schooling is of interest to us. We already know more than we need to know in order to do that. Whether or not we do it must finally depend on how we feel about the fact we haven't so far.

— *Ron Edmonds*

Average teachers teach because they love their subject. Good teachers teach because they love to teach. Great teachers teach because they love students.

—Todd Whitaker

If there is anything education does not lack today, it is critics.

—Nathan M. Pusey

Setting an example is not the main means of influencing another; it is the only means.

—Albert Einstein

If we don't model what we teach, then we are teaching something else.

—Author unknown

To arrive at the simple is difficult.

—Rashid Elisha

The best teachers make every decision based on what is best for their students.

—Al Burr

God doesn't look at how much we do, but with how much love we do it.

—Mother Theresa

A great teacher makes it cool to care.

—Todd Whitaker

One of the most important things we can teach our students is to pay attention: attention to people and attention to everything around them. There is so much to learn in life if we all just pay attention.

—Mary Beierl Charboneau

Great teachers ignore minor errors.

—Todd Whitaker

Always take your job seriously, never yourself.

*—Dwight D. Eisenhower,
quoting Fox Conner*

Real activities achieve real results.

—Dale Lumpa

The schools ain't what they used to be and never was.

—Will Rogers

Education's purpose is to replace an empty mind with an open one.

—Malcolm Forbes

Good teaching is more a giving of right questions than a giving of right answers.

—Josef Albers

Things turn out best for those who make the best of the way things turn out.

—Jack Buck

Of the 97 ways to learn anything, the most powerful way is to teach someone else.

—Author unknown

Ask your students to teach their parents something at least twice a week.

—Author unknown

Are you building student dependency or capacity?

—Author unknown

The best teachers are also learners, and the best learners are also teachers.

—Todd Whitaker

Teaching kids to count is fine, but teaching them what counts is best.

—Bob Talbert

You do not have to be kind to be a teacher, but you do have to be kind to be a good one.

—Todd Whitaker

To teach is to learn.

—Japanese proverb

There is no one best way to teach. If there were, we would all already be doing it.

—Todd Whitaker

Great teachers know that teaching can take place from behind a desk—just so it's the student's desk.

—Author unknown

Special teachers make students feel special.

—Dale Lumpa

It is a general insight, which merits more attention than it receives, that teaching should not be compared to filling a bottle with water but rather to helping a flower grow in its own way. As any good teacher knows, the methods of instruction and the range of material covered are matters of small importance as compared with the success in arousing the natural curiosity of the students and stimulating their interest in exploring on their own.

—Noam Chomsky

Luck is what happens when preparation meets opportunity.

—Darrell Royal

After teaching all day, if you didn't learn anything, you probably didn't teach anything either.

—Don Taylor

I'd rather have an apple on my desk than a BMW in my garage.

—Todd Whitaker

Tell me, and I forget. Show me, and I may not remember. Involve me, and I understand.

—Native American saying

Make certain that your students not only work hard, but enjoy their work.

—Author unknown

The bad teacher's words fall on his pupils like harsh rain; the good teacher's, as gently as the dew.

—Talmud

Teaching is helping young people believe the impossible is possible.

—Todd Whitaker

To know how to suggest is the great art of teaching.

—Henri Frederic Amiel

Students need to know why they are learning what they are learning.

—Dale Lumpa

The man who can make hard things easy is the educator.

—Ralph Waldo Emerson

Teachers learn from the discussions of their students.

—Rashi

We must teach our children to dream with their eyes open.

—Harry Edwards

The dream begins, most of the time, with a teacher who believes in you, who tugs and pushes and leads you on to the next plateau, sometimes poking you with a sharp stick called truth.

—Dan Rather

If teaching were easy, we wouldn't need teachers.

—Todd Whitaker

In the final analysis, it is not what you do for your children but what you have taught them to do for themselves that will make them successful human beings.

—Ann Landers

Act enthusiastic and you become enthusiastic.

—Dale Carnegie

The mediocre teacher tells. The good teacher explains. The superior teacher demonstrates. The great teacher inspires.

—William Arthur Ward

He who opens a school door, closes a prison.

—Victor Hugo

Education is not the filling of a pail, but the lighting of a fire.

—William Butler Yeats

The mind is not a vessel to be filled, but a fire to be ignited.

—Plutarch

Teaching isn't strip mining; it's cultivating.

—Todd Whitaker

Effective teaching may be the hardest job there is.

—William Glasser

Students aren't learning resistant; they are poor teacher resistant.

—Todd Whitaker

Everything should be made as simple as possible, but not simpler.

—Albert Einstein

The greatest sign of success for a teacher is to be able to say, "The children are now working as if I did not exist."

—Maria Montessori

The beginning is the most important part of the work.

—Plato

To teach is to learn twice.

—Joseph Joubert

Each student effects a strength or weakness within you.

—Todd Whitaker

Give me a fish and I eat for a day. Teach me to fish and I eat for a lifetime.

—Chinese proverb

Experience is a good teacher, as long as it is good experience.

—Todd Whitaker

I am not teaching these thinking strategies because they are the latest trend, I am teaching them because they work.

—Mary Brinks

How to tell students what to look for without telling them what to see is the dilemma of teaching.

—Lascelles Abercrombie

Always treat your students as if their parents were in the room.

—Todd Whitaker

Echoes

Real Quotes from Real Students

- *I like science because my teacher makes it fun and cool.*

- *I love everything about school because the teachers are everything.*

- *I love my Tech Arts teacher because we build stuff and he cares about us.*

- *I want to teach high school history or geography because I like to help people. I also want to show my old teachers that I'm not a disappointment.*

- *The best things about school are my locker, learning to read in first grade, and getting a high five from my principal.*

3 Students— The Core of Every Apple

My goal as an educator is that every afternoon, kids are chomping at the bit to come back tomorrow.

—Dale Lumpa

The mind of a child is fascinating, for it looks on old things with new eyes.

—F. Scott Fitzgerald

Students are seldom late for classes when they feel they might miss something of value.

—Todd Whitaker

For many students, their teachers may be the only adult with whom they have a meaningful conversation all day.

—Vickie Gill

Don't laugh at a youth for his affectations; he is only trying on one face after another to find a face of his own.

—Logan Pearsall Smith

Let us always be open to the miracle of the second chance.

—David Stiel

No one like you was ever born or ever will be.

—Constance Foster

You don't have to like the students; you just have to act as if you like them. The reason is simple: If you don't act as if you like them, then it doesn't matter how much you like them. And if you act as if you like them, then it doesn't matter whether you like them.

—Todd Whitaker

We must have...a place where children can have a whole group of adults they can trust.

—Margaret Mead

We cannot always build the future for our youth, but we can build our youth for the future.

—Franklin D. Roosevelt

The children of today are too much in love with luxury. They have bad manners, flout authority, and have no respect for their elders. I can only fear what kind of awful creatures they will be when they grow up.

—Socrates

School is a place where children come to watch adults work!

—Madeline Hunter

The teachers' best mirror is their students.

—Todd Whitaker

It's great to be great, but it's greater to be human.

—Will Rogers

When I was a boy of fourteen, my father was so ignorant I could hardly stand to have the old man around. But when I got to be twenty-one, I was astonished at how much the old man had learned in seven years.

—Mark Twain

We cannot choose which students we most influence; only they can choose who will most influence them.

—Todd Whitaker

Likely as not, the child you can do the least with will do the most to make you proud.

—Mignon McLaughlin

Know that a student's perception is a student's reality.

—Dale Lumpa

A happy child can learn.

—Author unknown

Nothing is so simple that it cannot be misunderstood.

—Jr. Teague

Children need love, especially when they do not deserve it.

—Harold S. Hulbert

Children are the living messages we send to a time we will not see.

—Neil Postman

Let others praise ancient times; I am glad I was born in these.

—Ovid

Children today are tyrants. They contradict their parents, gobble their food, and tyrannize their teachers.

—Socrates

Students we want the least need us the most.

—Todd Whitaker

I am not young enough to know everything.

—Oscar Wilde

When you're young, the silliest notions seem the greatest achievements.

—Pearl Bailey

A boy becomes an adult three years before his parents think he does, and about two years after he thinks he does.

—Lewis B. Hershey

Amongst democratic nations, each new generation is a new people.

—Alexis de Tocqueville

Each generation criticizes the unconscious assumptions made by its parents.

—Alfred North Whitehead

Everyone believes in his youth that the world really began with him, and that all merely exists for his sake.

—Goethe

No young man believes he shall ever die.

—William Hazlitt

Youth, even in its sorrows, always has a brilliancy of its own.

—Victor Hugo

Great Quotes for Great Educators

In a great teacher's classroom, every student feels like the favorite.

—Todd Whitaker

It is an illusion that youth is happy, an illusion of those who have lost it.

—W. Somerset Maugham

It is a happy talent to know how to play.

—Ralph Waldo Emerson

That energy which makes a child hard to manage is the energy which afterward makes him a manager of life.

—Henry Ward Beecher

Children are all foreigners.

—Ralph Waldo Emerson

I have learned much from my teachers, and from my colleagues more than from my teachers, and from my students more than from all.

—Haggadah

Aerodynamically, the bumblebee shouldn't be able to fly, but the bumblebee doesn't know that, so it goes on flying anyway.

—Mary Kay Ash

A child's life is like a piece of paper on which every passerby leaves a mark.

—Chinese proverb

I see the mind of the five-year-old as a volcano with two vents: destructiveness and creativeness.

—Sylvia Ashton-Warner

The best teachers have the best students—every year.

—Todd Whitaker

Only little children and old folks tell the truth.

—Sarah Louise Delany

The good old days were never that good, believe me. The good new days are today and better days are coming tomorrow. Our greatest songs are still unsung.

—Hubert Humphrey

It is as important for children to grow up fit as it is to grow up smart.

—Arnold Schwarzenegger

Great achievers are often great troublemakers. Don't they have to be, at least some of the time?

—Annie Leibowitz

As I see it, if you're quiet, you're not living. You've got to be noisy, or at least your thoughts should be noisy and colorful and lively.

—Mel Brooks

Anyone can teach algebra. The challenge is to teach algebra students.

—Todd Whitaker

There are days these kids drive me crazy—I just love them all!

—Mary Vincent

Echoes

Real Quotes from Real Students

- *I like the special days at school. Crazy Hair Day and Hat Day really make me feel special.*

- *My favorite teacher had a wild imagination and always took time for me.*

- *My preschool teacher gave me lots of hugs even if she was having a bad day.*

- *The three things I like about school are all the teachers because they clearly explain difficult techniques. I like all the activities because they give you an opportunity to discover what you like to do and who you are. Third, I enjoy the school food because it doesn't smell like it will kill you if you take a bite.*

4

Learning for Life

A teacher never stops learning,
and a learner never stops teaching.

—Todd Whitaker

The mind, once expanded to the dimensions of larger ideas, never returns to its original size.

—Oliver W. Holmes

The principal goal of education is to create people who are capable of doing new things, not simply repeating what other generations have done—people who are creative, inventive discoverers.

—Jean Piaget

Not everything that can be counted counts, and not everything that counts can be counted.

—Albert Einstein

They know enough who know how to learn.

—Henry Brooks Adams

Learning is not something like chicken pox, a childhood disease that makes you itch for a while and then leaves you immune for the rest of your life.

—Roland Barth

Look for learning worth remembering for a lifetime.

—Author unknown

That which is unique and worthwhile in each of us is revealed to us in flashes. Unless we learn to catch the flashes, we are without growth or exhilaration.

—Author unknown

It takes courage to grow up and turn out to be who you really are.

—e e cummings

Unless you try to do something beyond what you have already mastered, you will never grow.

—Ralph Waldo Emerson

I find the great thing in this world is not so much where we stand, as in what direction we are moving—we must sail sometimes with the wind and sometimes against it—but we must sail, and not drift, nor lie at anchor.

—Oliver Wendell Holmes

If you want to feel secure, do what you already know how to do. If you want to be a true professional and continue to grow . . . go to the cutting-edge of your competence, which means a temporary loss of security. So whenever you don't quite know what you're doing, know that you are growing.

—Madeline Hunter

Grand adventures await those willing to turn the corner.

—Author unknown

A definition of school is "four walls surrounding the future."

—Roland Barth

The big thing is not what happens to us in life, but what we do about what happens to us.

—George Allen

Life can only be understood backward, but must be lived forward.

—Søren Kierkegaard

Sixty years ago I knew everything; now I know nothing; education is a progressive discovery of our own ignorance.

—Will Durant

Maybe the only thing better than teaching is learning.

—Todd Whitaker

Education can't make us all leaders, but it can teach us which leader to follow.

—Author unknown

All of us have two educations: one which we receive from others; another, and most valuable, which we give ourselves.

—John Randolph

To really know a man, observe his behavior with a woman, a flat tire, and a child.

—Author unknown

Failure to prepare is preparing to fail.

—John Wooden

Having a sense of humor does not require being funny. It only requires being fun.

—Todd Whitaker

An education system isn't worth a great deal if it teaches young people how to make a living and doesn't teach them how to live.

—Author unknown

I hear, and I forget. I see, and I remember. I do, and I understand.

—Chinese proverb

Negative attitudes are a sort of poison.

—Fran Tarkenton

Ignorance—the root and the stem of every evil.

—Plato

A fanatic is one who can't change his mind and won't change the subject.

—Winston Churchill

No one can make you feel inferior without your consent.

—Eleanor Roosevelt

Excellence is doing ordinary things extraordinarily well.

—John W. Gardner

He who is not courageous enough to take risks will accomplish nothing in life.

—Muhammad Ali

When all is said and done, as a rule, more is said than done.

—Lou Holtz

Talent is God-given, be humble; fame is man-given, be thankful; conceit is self-given, be careful.

—John Wooden

Learning happens when your head, hands, and heart are involved.

—Author unknown

Knowledge is power.

—Francis Bacon

Education is not preparation for life; education is life itself.

—John Dewey

Tomorrow comes to us at midnight very clean. It's perfect when it arrives, and it pushes itself in our hands and hopes we've learnt something from yesterday.

—John Wayne

I don't divide the world into the weak and the strong, or the successes and the failures, those who make it or those who don't. I divide the world into learners and non-learners.

—Benjamin Barber

Ain't no man can avoid being born average, but there ain't no man got to be common.

—Satchel Paige

We have to abandon the idea that schooling is something restricted to youth. How can it be, in a world where half the things a man knows at 20 are no longer true at 40—and half the things he knows at 40 hadn't been discovered when he was 20?

—*Arthur C. Clarke*

Don't measure yourself by what you have accomplished, but by what you should have accomplished with your ability.

—*John Wooden*

Experience is the name everyone gives to their mistakes.

—*Oscar Wilde*

What luck for rulers, that men do not think.

—*Adolf Hitler*

Ability may get you to the top, but it takes character to keep you there.

—John Wooden

A thought which does not result in an action is nothing much, and an action which does not proceed from a thought is nothing at all.

—Georges Bernanos

What is the hardest task in the world? To think.

—Ralph Waldo Emerson

There is nothing so powerful as truth, and often nothing so strange.

—Daniel Webster

Everyone is a fool for at least five minutes every day. Wisdom consists in not exceeding the limit.

—Elbert Hubbard

Education is not a product: mark, diploma, job, money—in that order; it is a process, a never-ending one.

—Bel Kaufman

Luck is the residue of design.

—Branch Rickey

It is not enough to have a good mind; the main thing is to use it well.

—René Descartes

You have learned something. That always feels at first as if you had lost something.

—George Bernard Shaw

All men by nature desire to know.

—Aristotle

In theory, there is no difference between theory and practice. In practice, there is.

—Yogi Berra

The greatest mistake a person can make is to be afraid of making one.

—Elbert Hubbard

Education is simply the soul of a society as it passes from one generation to another.

—Gilbert K. Chesterton

True happiness involves the full use of one's power and talents.

—John W. Gardner

Education is a better safeguard of liberty than a standing army.

—Edward Everett

Education's purpose is to replace an empty mind with an open one.

—Malcolm S. Forbes

Why should society feel responsible only for the education of children, and not for the education of all adults of every age?

—Erich Fromm

The object of education is to prepare the young to educate themselves throughout their lives.

—Robert M. Hutchins

I honestly think it is better to be a failure at something you love than to be a success at something you hate.

—George Burns

Some people drink from the fountain of knowledge, others just gargle.

—Robert Anthony

Great Quotes for Great Educators

The society which scorns excellence in plumbing as a humble activity and tolerates shoddiness in philosophy because it is an exalted activity will have neither good plumbing nor good philosophy: neither its pipes nor its theories will hold water.

—John W. Gardner

Nothing is more responsible for the good old days than a bad memory.

—Franklin Pierce Adams

By viewing the old we learn the new.

—Chinese proverb

You can observe a lot by just watching.

—Yogi Berra

One can think effectively only when one is willing to endure suspense and to undergo the trouble of searching.

—*John Dewey*

Anyone who stops learning is old, whether at twenty or eighty. Anyone who keeps learning stays young.

—*Henry Ford*

When inspiration does not come to me, I go halfway to meet it.

—*Sigmund Freud*

It's what you learn after you know it all that counts.

—*Harry S. Truman*

Human history becomes more and more a race between education and catastrophe.

—H. G. Wells

If one test can determine our ability to succeed, then why don't all employers give their applicants that one test?

—Todd Whitaker

You're never too old to become younger.

—Mae West

Learning is by nature curiosity.

—Philo

It is better to know nothing than to learn nothing.

—Hebrew Proverb

A man is not old as long as he is seeking something.

—Jean Rostand

In the beginner's mind there are many possibilities; in the expert's there are few.

—Shunryu Suzuki-roshi

Live every day like it's your last, cause one day you're gonna be right.

—Ray Charles

The most wasted of all days is that in which we have not laughed.

—Sébastien-Roch Nicolas de Chamfort

Courage can achieve anything.

—Sam Houston

Echoes

Real Quotes from Real Students

- *Mrs. Kokenburger touched my life. I can't put into words how much she influenced me.*

- *My fifth-grade teacher was real cool and she had the best stories about her life.*

- *My favorite teacher gives us room to grow and to give opinions. She really listens.*

- *My favorite teacher helped me with new friends.*

- *My teacher said I will make a difference in the world.*

5 The Gift of Literacy

Teaching students to read and write is a teacher's job. Teaching students to love reading and writing is a teacher's gift.

—Dale Lumpa

We shouldn't teach great books; we should teach a love of reading.

—B. F. Skinner

The man who does not read good books has no advantage over the man who cannot read them.

—Mark Twain

'Tis the good reader that makes the good book; in every book he finds passages which seem confidences or asides hidden from all else and unmistakably meant for his ear.

—Ralph Waldo Emerson

When you read a classic, you do not see more in the book than you did before; you see more in you than there was before.

—Clifton Fadiman

Good teachers prepare students for the test. Great teachers prepare students for their life.

—Todd Whitaker

I cannot live without books.

—Thomas Jefferson

I would never read a book if it were possible for me to talk half an hour with the man who wrote it.

—Woodrow Wilson

The remarkable thing about Shakespeare is that he really is very good, in spite of all the people who say he is very good.

—Robert Graves

Reading is to the mind what exercise is to the body.

—Joseph Addison

Teachers can become part of a student's life script.

—Vickie Gill

A house without books is like a room without windows.

—Horace Mann

Writing comes more easily if you have something to say.

—Sholem Asch

A real book is not one that we read, but one that reads us.

—W. H. Auden

We don't teach students to read so that they can read worksheets.

—Todd Whitaker

Is sloppiness in speech caused by ignorance or apathy? I don't know and I don't care.

—William Safire

The limits of your language are the limits of your world.

—Ludwig Wittgenstein

Your classroom must reward imagination as much as memory.

—Gary Phillips

A good book is like an unreachable itch. You just can't leave it alone.

—Laura Bush

You cannot open a book without learning something.

—Chinese proverb

It is not how much material we cover—it is how much we uncover.

—Todd Whitaker

It is better to know some of the questions than all of the answers.

—*James Thurber*

It takes a great man to make a good listener.

—*Arthur Helps*

In the fields of observation, chance favors only the prepared mind.

—*Louis Pasteur*

You will never have any mental muscle if you don't have any heavy stuff to pick up.

—*Diane Lane*

The illiterate of the 21st century will not be those who cannot read and write, but those who cannot learn, unlearn, and relearn.

—Alvin Toffler

"I don't think, I know!" —A teacher to a student
"I don't think I know either!" —A student to a teacher

Your students may forget what you know about the subject, but they'll never forget what you understand about them.

—Todd Whitaker

People without information cannot act responsibly. People with information are compelled to act responsibly.

—Ken Blanchard

The only thing that increases because of worksheets is papercuts.

—Todd Whitaker

Echoes

Real Quotes from Real Students

- *Ms. Weiss opened up writing into my life. I never liked writing until third grade because it bored me. But she showed me how awesome it can be to put down ideas on paper. She helped me get into the city writing contest, and I almost won! I want to be a writing teacher!*

- *My favorite teacher was, and still is, Mr. Goodman. He let me express myself through writing and debate like no one else ever has.*

- *I learned from my homeroom teacher that the greatest and most valuable thing a person can own is the gift of knowledge.*

6 If at First You Don't Succeed

We are never sorry when we do our best. We are only sorry when we do not.

—Todd Whitaker

Whether you think you can or you think you can't, you are right.

—Henry Ford

Sometimes, it's more fun to mow where the grass is long.

—Author unknown

A little success sure makes you try harder.

—Todd Whitaker

One may walk over the highest mountain one step at a time.

—John Wanamaker

Winning isn't everything—but making the effort to win is.

                         —Vince Lombardi

Never give up, never give up, never, ever give up!

                         —Winston Churchill

Tough times don't last long, but tough people do.

                         —Darryl Kile

Those who have a why will always find a how.

                         —Author unknown

If you want to make an easy job seem mighty hard, just keep putting off doing it!

—Olin Miller

Treating unequals equally is no justice.

—Gary Phillips

Put your mules in horse races. You know they can't win, but at least they can see how fast four-legged animals can run.

—Author unknown

When you make a mistake, there are only three things you should ever do about it: (1) admit it; (2) learn from it; and (3) don't repeat it.

—Paul "Bear" Bryant

If you are already in a hole, stop digging.

—Author unknown

The more difficult a victory, the greater the happiness in winning.

—Pelé

Adversity causes some men to break and others to break records.

—William Ward

It is never too late to be what you might have become.

—George Eliot

Nothing great was ever achieved without enthusiasm.

—Ralph Waldo Emerson

The greatest accomplishment is not in never falling, but in rising again after you fall.

—Vince Lombardi

Most people don't aim too high and miss; they aim too low and hit.

—Old adage

Great teachers see challenging students as a reason to try that much harder.

—Todd Whitaker

I've never known anybody to achieve anything without overcoming adversity.

—Lou Holtz

I have always struggled to achieve excellence. One thing that cycling has taught me is that if you can achieve something without a struggle it's not going to be satisfying.

—Greg LeMond

What you do speaks so loud that I cannot hear what you say.

—Ralph Waldo Emerson

The man who can drive himself further once the effort gets painful is the man who will win.

—Roger Bannister

Eighty percent of success is showing up.

—Woody Allen

There are no shortcuts to the future.

—Todd Whitaker

The difference between a successful person and others is not a lack of strength, not a lack of knowledge, but rather a lack of will.

—Vince Lombardi

I find that the harder I work, the more luck I seem to have.

—Thomas Jefferson

You can't get much done in life if you only work on the days you feel good.

—Jerry West

Success isn't a result of spontaneous combustion. You must set yourself on fire.

—Arnold H. Glasow

Nobody who ever gave his best regretted it.

—George Halas

Problems are the price you pay for progress.

—Branch Rickey

Great Quotes for Great Educators

The more F's we give, the more we have failed.

—Todd Whitaker

When one door of happiness closes, another opens; but often we look so long at the closed door that we do not see the one which has been opened for us.

—Helen Keller

Do not let what you cannot do interfere with what you can do.

—John Wooden

Character consists of what you do on the third and fourth tries.

—James Michener

A journey of a thousand miles must begin with a single step.

—*Chinese proverb*

The problem is not there are problems. The problem is expecting otherwise and thinking that having problems is a problem.

—*Theodore Rubin*

The key to teaching is not expecting perfection.

—*Todd Whitaker*

Don't try to perform beyond your abilities—but never perform below them.

—*Frank Robinson*

In life you are given two ends, one to think with and the other to sit on. Your success in life depends on which end you use the most. Heads you win, tails you lose.

—*Conrad Burns*

Hard work is often the easy work you did not do at the proper time.

—*Bernard Meltzer*

Use what talent you possess. The woods would be very silent if no birds sang except those that sang best.

—*Henry Van Dyke*

Beyond talent lie all the usual words: discipline, love, luck—but, most of all, endurance.

—*James Arthur Baldwin*

Character cannot be developed in ease and quiet. Only through experience of trial and suffering can the soul be strengthened, ambition inspired, and success achieved.

—Helen Keller

Rest awhile and run a mile.

—Palsgrave

Only the mediocre are always at their best.

—Jean Giraudoux

A good man is always a beginner.

—Martial

To win, you have to risk loss.

     —Jean-Claude Killy

The only thing some tests measure is your patience.

     —Todd Whitaker

There is no substitute for hard work.

     —Thomas Edison

Truth is what stands the test of experience.

     —Albert Einstein

Genius is one percent inspiration and ninety-nine percent perspiration.

—Thomas Edison

He who limps is still walking.

—Stanislaw Lec

A smooth sea never made a skillful mariner.

—English proverb

If at first you don't succeed, you're running about average.

—M. H. Alderson

In order to succeed, your desire for success should be greater than your fear of failure.

—Bill Cosby

We have nothing to fear but fear itself.

—Franklin D. Roosevelt

Success is simply a matter of luck. Ask any failure.

—Earl Wilson

You never really lose until you stop trying.

—Mike Ditka

I couldn't wait for success, so I went ahead without it.

—Jonathan Winters

We are all faced with a series of great opportunities, brilliantly disguised as insoluble problems.

—John W. Gardner

Never quit. It is the easiest cop-out in the world. Set a goal and don't quit until you attain it. When you do attain it, set another goal, and don't quit until you reach it. Never quit.

—Paul "Bear" Bryant

Opportunity is missed by most people because it is dressed in overalls and looks like work.

—Thomas Edison

Confidence is the most valuable gift we can give.

—Todd Whitaker

Oh yes you can!

—Author unknown

Never deprive anyone of hope. It might be all that they have.

—J. Browne

If you always think the problem was last year's teacher, there is a pretty good chance it is this year's teacher.

—Todd Whitaker

Echoes

Real Quotes from Real Students

- *In second grade, Mrs. Bade made me realize that trying new things was good.*

- *My favorite teacher taught me how to learn from my mistakes and not to be afraid of making them.*

- *My favorite teacher was my fifth-grade teacher who made me believe in myself.*

- *My favorite teachers always made it OK to try new stuff.*

7

Managing with Class

*We can never control a classroom
until we control ourselves.*

—Todd Whitaker

Catch them doing something right! If you can catch people doing something well, no matter how small it may seem, and positively reinforce them for doing it, they will continue to grow in a positive direction.

—Ken Blanchard

In the great teacher's classroom, very little happens at random.

—Todd Whitaker

Raise the praise, minimize the criticize!

—Author unknown

Students will remember how we treated them long after they forget what we taught them.

—Author unknown

To handle yourself, use your head. To handle others, use your heart.

—Donald Laird

It is impossible to praise too much as long as it is authentic.

—Ben Bissell

Which comment is more likely to keep you on a diet: "You're looking good," or "It's about time"?

—Todd Whitaker

Temper is the one thing you can't get rid of by losing it.

—Jack Nicholson (as Dr. Buddy in "Anger Management")

I can live for two months on a good compliment.

—Mark Twain

If you compliment someone often enough, that person will begin to think you have incredibly good taste.

—Todd Whitaker

Knowledge which is acquired under compulsion obtains no hold on the mind.

—Plato

In discipline, poor managers react by looking to fix the students, and good managers prevent by looking to fix themselves.

—Todd Whitaker

It is a funny thing about life; if you refuse to accept anything but the best, you very often get it.

—W. Somerset Maugham

With good classroom management you may still not have learning, but without good classroom management you never will.

—Todd Whitaker

If you don't have the time to do it right, when will you have time to do it over?

—Author unknown

The teacher who says, "I've told you a dozen times . . ." is the slow learner.

—Todd Whitaker

Don't take it personally. Don't make it personal.

—Author unknown

If the mailman stopped for every barking dog, he'd never finish his route.

—P. Allen

If punishment led to improvement, then many of the kids we work with would already be geniuses.

—Author unknown

If a student is misbehaving, the teacher needs to make sure that the student is the only one misbehaving.

—Todd Whitaker

Managing a difficult person first requires you to manage yourself.

—Elaine McEwan

There are two kinds of leaders—those who call the shots and those who dodge the bullets.

—Author unknown

Your least favorite student probably has a least favorite teacher.

—Todd Whitaker

Sometimes when I consider what tremendous consequences come from little things . . . I am tempted to think there are no little things.

—Bruce Barton

No act of kindness, no matter how small, is ever wasted.

—Aesop

We smile at every student we pass in the hallway because it might mean something to them.

—Todd Whitaker

An educator never says what he himself thinks, but only that which he thinks it is good for those whom he is educating to hear.

—Nietzsche

Students emulate teachers' actions more often than listen to their words.

—Todd Whitaker

Children need models rather than critics.

—Joseph Joubert

Never yell at a student. The students we are most tempted to treat that way have already been treated that way—their whole life.

—Todd Whitaker

A torn jacket is soon mended, but hard words bruise the heart of a child.

—Henry Wadsworth Longfellow

The only thing harder than managing a bunch of students is to do it while driving a bus.

—Todd Whitaker

The art of being wise is knowing what to overlook.

—William James

Reprove a friend in secret, but praise him before others.

—Leonardo da Vinci

If you don't smile until Thanksgiving, your students never will.

—Todd Whitaker

Good classroom management has much more to do with class than it does with management.

—Todd Whitaker

Echoes

Real Quotes from Real Students

♦ *What are the rules of this place?*
  —A first-grader

♦ *I love my locker and my teachers.*

♦ *Ms. Bussell stopped some bullies when they were making me feel bad.*

♦ *My first-grade teacher was my favorite. She was always very kind and seemed like she was willing to help me no matter what the situation was.*

♦ *I want to be a teacher because I want to make kids feel happy and not make them sit through stuff that does not make sense.*

8 *R-E-S-P-E-C-T*

The only way to teach respect is to model it.

—Todd Whitaker

In all student-teacher interactions, there needs to be at least one adult—and it works best if it is the teacher.

—Todd Whitaker

Make each day your masterpiece.

—John Wooden

As a teacher, you are remembered forever, but how you are remembered is up to you.

—Vickie Gill

I'm not concerned with your liking or disliking me. All I ask is that you respect me as a human being.

—Jackie Robinson

Politeness can have an almost magical effect on people.

—*Caitlin Davies*

I am for what works. If blaming, whining, and complaining worked, I would blame, whine, and complain. I have yet to see those things work, so I don't do them.

—**Dale Lumpa**

Even if they aren't listening, quality teachers still act as if they are.

—**Todd Whitaker**

Teachers get what teachers model.

—*Author unknown*

Whining is worthless; caring is keen.

—Todd Whitaker

Tap into people's dignity, and they will do anything for you. Ignore it, and they won't lift a finger.

—Thomas Friedman

No matter how busy you are, you must take time to make the other person feel important.

—Mary Kay Ash

Some teachers bring their students up. Others let them down.

—Todd Whitaker

Wherever I look, I see signs of the commandment to honor one's parents and nowhere of a commandment that calls for the respect of a child.

—Alice Miller

Listening to kids teaches us more than talking to kids.

—Dale Lumpa

The secret of education is respecting the pupil.

—Ralph Waldo Emerson

Make a kid feel stupid and he'll act stupider.

—John Caldwell Holt

Teachers who lose their heads lose their students.

—Todd Whitaker

We should not be speaking to, but with.

—Noam Chomsky

Treat people as if they were what they ought to be and you will help them become what they are capable of becoming.

—Johann Wolfgang von Goethe

If we all lived the way we expected our neighbors to live, we'd have us a world full of saints.

—Will Rogers

We have all known store clerks who treated us rudely because the last person treated them rudely . . . and we have all known store clerks who haven't.

—Todd Whitaker

If you tell the truth, you don't need a long memory.

—Jesse Ventura

The smallest deed is greater than the grandest intention.

—Author unknown, quoted by Patti LaBelle in "LaBelle Cuisine"

You can't see the world through a mirror.

—Avril Lavigne

If you want to find out whether what you are doing for kids is good, just ask them.

—Dale Lumpa

When you reach for the stars you may not quite get one, but you won't come up with a handful of mud either.

—Leo Burnett

Great teachers do not act important; they make their students feel important.

—Todd Whitaker

Arguing with a student is like mud-wrestling a pig. You both get muddy, but the pig loves it.

—Author unknown

Speak when you are angry and you will make the best speech you will ever regret.

—Ambrose Bierce

Children have never been very good at listening to their elders, but they have never failed to imitate them.

—James Arthur Baldwin

We do not earn respect. It is given as a gift. What we do with it is up to us.

—Todd Whitaker

The more a child feels valued, the better the child's values.

—Author unknown

When I was young there was no respect for the young, and now that I am old there is no respect for the old. I missed out coming and going.

—J. B. Priestley

Instead of putting students in their place, put yourself in the student's place.

—Todd Whitaker

Getting students to like you is merely the other side of you liking them.

—Author unknown

Treat every student like your favorite student.

—Todd Whitaker

You prove your worth with your actions, not with your mouth.

—Jean Paul Richter

Students who feel special act special. Students who feel stupid act stupid.

—Gary Phillips

Treat every student with respect and dignity every day. After all, how many days do you want students treating you with respect and dignity?

—Todd Whitaker

Great teachers treat their students the way their best teacher treated them.

—Al Burr

Treat all students as if they were good.

—Todd Whitaker

Growing up in a loving home is the best break anyone can have.

—Walter Mondale

A student needs to be loved the most when he deserves to be loved the least.

—Author unknown

Sarcasm: Humiliating someone in front of their peers under the guise of humor.

—Author unknown

Echoes

Real Quotes from Real Students

- *My favorite teacher makes me feel like I am her only student.*

- *I like my teacher because she likes me.*

- *I like my teacher this year because she is cool and she is very kind and doesn't get mad so fast like a regular teacher.*

- *My favorite teacher was patient even when I was not.*

- *My favorite was my first-grade teacher because she thanked me for being in her class every day.*

- *My favorite teacher always has time for me.*

9 *Leading the Learning*

You should never feel guilty about doing what is best for the young people in your buildings. You should only feel guilty if you don't.

Todd Whitaker

When the best leader's work is done the people say, "We did it ourselves."

—Lao-Tzu

Leadership is the art of getting someone else to do something you want done because he wants to do it.

—Dwight D. Eisenhower

The best principals are not heroes; they are hero makers.

—Roland Barth

If the best teacher in a school does not think something is a good idea, then it probably isn't.

—Todd Whitaker

A person always doing his or her best becomes a natural leader, just by example.

—Joe DiMaggio

There is something that is much more scarce, something finer far, something rarer than ability. It is the ability to recognize ability.

—Elbert Hubbard

When the principal sneezes, the whole school catches a cold.

—Todd Whitaker

Managing is like holding a dove in your hand. Squeeze too hard and you kill it; not hard enough and it flies away.

—Tommy Lasorda

Great Quotes for Great Educators

The best public relations are based on good deeds.

—Stanley Marcus

In many ways the saying "Know thyself" is lacking. Better to know other people.

—Menander

The worse the news, the more effort must go into delivering it.

—Author unknown

Never deliver bad news in writing.

—Author unknown

What gets measured gets done.

—Tom Peters

A school without vision is a vacuum inviting intrusion.

—Roland Barth

Schools are so overwhelmed with new ideas that it is difficult to find the core inside the apple.

—Todd Whitaker

If I had six hours to chop down a tree, I'd spend the first four sharpening the axe.

—Abraham Lincoln

If you fail to satisfy people's craving for communication, the rumor mill will fill the void.

—Author unknown

A leader is interested in finding the best way—not in having his own way.

—John Wooden

The principal is the head learner, engaging in, displaying, and modeling the behavior we expect and hope teachers and students will adopt.

—Roland Barth

We ask others their opinion precisely because they have one.

—Todd Whitaker

Be <u>hard</u> on issues and <u>soft</u> on people.

—Author unknown

Vision is the world's most desperate need. There are no hopeless situations, only people who think hopelessly.

—Winifred Newman

People may not do what's expected, but they will do what is inspected.

—Author unknown

Some principals look for candidates who are a good match—teachers who will fit in and become like their school. Great principals have a different goal: to have the school become more like the new teacher. Otherwise, we are hiring the wrong people.

—Todd Whitaker

Empowerment is the art of increasing the competence and capability of others by endowing them with a sense of self-worth and potency.

—Thomas Harvey and Bonita Drolet

Seek first to understand and then to be understood.

—Stephen Covey

People don't always want to move and shake when you do, because they don't share your values.

—Author unknown

As a principal, never be defensive, but never be offensive.

—Author unknown

Leaders predict and prevent. Amateurs react and repair.

—Author unknown

People resent others being valued only when they do not feel valued themselves.

—Todd Whitaker

I hold it more important to have the players' confidence than their affection.

—Vince Lombardi

Even if great teachers cost more, poor teachers still cost the most.

—Todd Whitaker

It's easy to get the players. Getting them to play together, that's the hard part.

—*Casey Stengel*

Power in organization is the capacity generated by relationships.

—*Margaret Wheatley*

A prime function of a leader is to keep hope alive.

—*John W. Gardner*

If you've got enough enthusiasm so it infects other people, everybody is going to do better.

—*Willie Mays*

There is no such thing as constructive criticism.

—Todd Whitaker

Act as if everyone were related to you.

—Navajo saying

Always ask yourself—is this decision best for kids?

—Dale Lumpa

Leadership is being visible when things are going awry and invisible when they are working well.

—Tom Peters

A leader is a person you would follow to a place you wouldn't go by yourself.

—Joel A. Barker

Leadership is getting someone to do what they don't want to do, to achieve what they want to achieve.

—Tom Landry

I start with the premise that the function of leadership is to produce more leaders, not more followers.

—Ralph Nader

Good leadership consists in showing average people how to do the work of superior people.

—John D. Rockefeller

Good leaders make people feel that they're at the very heart of things, not at the periphery.

—Warren G. Bennis

The great leaders are like the best conductors—they reach beyond the notes to reach the magic in the players.

—Blaine Lee

Vision without action is merely a dream. Action without vision just passes the time. Vision with action can change the world.

—Joel A. Barker

There are two ways of being creative. One can sing and dance. Or one can create an environment in which singers and dancers flourish.

—Warren G. Bennis

Great Quotes for Great Educators

Pull the string, and it will follow wherever you wish. Push it, and it will go nowhere at all.

—Dwight D. Eisenhower

You can't fatten the cattle by weighing them. You have to feed them.

—Paul D. Houston

Always be smarter than the people who hire you.

—Lena Horne

A good leader inspires men to have confidence in him; a great leader inspires them to have confidence in themselves.

—E. C. McKenzie

What is the use of running when we are not on the right road?

—German proverb

If you want work well done, select a busy man. The other kind has no time.

—Elbert Hubbard

Bad administration, to be sure, can destroy good policy; but good administration can never save bad policy.

—Adlai Stevenson

When in doubt, tell the truth.

—Mark Twain

Great Quotes for Great Educators

The one important thing I have learned over the years is the difference between taking one's work seriously and taking one's self seriously. The first is imperative and the second is disastrous.

—Margot Fonteyn

One of the tests of leadership is the ability to recognize a problem before it becomes an emergency.

—Arnold H. Glasow

Leaders come in many forms, with many styles and diverse qualities. There are quiet leaders and leaders one can hear in the next county. Some find strength in eloquence, some in judgment, some in courage.

—John W. Gardner

Our tendency to create heroes rarely jibes with the reality that most nontrivial problems require collective solutions.

—Warren G. Bennis

A good leader take a little more than his share of the blame, a little less than his share of the credit.

—Arnold H. Glasow

Hard work today makes for easier tomorrows.

—Dale Lumpa

The quality of a leader is reflected in the standards they set for themselves.

—Ray Kroc

Great Quotes for Great Educators

When you get right down to it, one of the most important tasks of a leader is to eliminate his people's excuse for failure.

—Robert Townsend

Always understand the source before reacting.

—Dale Lumpa

The path is the goal.

—Chögyam Trungpa

Well done is better than well said.

—Ben Franklin

Leadership is not magnetic personality—that can just as well be a glib tongue. It is not "making friends and influencing people"—that is flattery. Leadership is lifting a person's vision to higher sights, the raising of a person's performance to a higher standard, the building of a personality beyond its normal limitations.

—Peter F. Drucker

There is a 1 to 1 relationship between student achievement and principal instructional leadership.

—Richard Andrews

A leader looks for opportunities to find someone doing something right.

—Author unknown

If people don't have their own vision, all they can do is "sign up" for someone else's. The result is compliance, not commitment.

—*Peter Senge*

A principal is a model without a runway.

—*Todd Whitaker*

Echoes

Real Quotes from Real Students

- *Did you know my teacher did not like math either? But he still is good at it and it helps his life.*

- *Ms. Lewis lets us learn with her during lunch.*

- *My favorite math lesson was when my teacher let me add corn and chicken nuggets during Lunch Bunch.*

- *I feel good when I get it.*

10 The Winds of Change

To learn to fly, you have to leave the ground. You can't taxi forever.

Todd Whitaker

People who are only good with hammers see every problem as a nail.

—Abraham Maslow

Sacred cows make the best hamburger.

—Mark Twain

In times of change, the learner inherits the earth, while the learned are beautifully prepared for a world that no longer exists.

—Eric Hoffer

The only behavior we can change is our own.

—Todd Whitaker

Few men during their lifetime come any-where near exhausting the resources dwell-ing within them. There are deep wells of strength that are never used.

—Richard E. Byrd

In schools, treading water is no longer an option. School people must either propel themselves in some direction, be towed, or sink.

—Roland Barth

Outstanding teachers make it safe to take risks.

—Todd Whitaker

Move from teachers as informers to teach-ers as transformers.

—Author unknown

Schools can no longer select the best and forget the rest.

—Author unknown

Today's problems come from yesterday's solutions.

—Peter Senge

Never do more of anything unless you have the courage to declare what you will do less of.

—Author unknown

Creating a better future starts with the ability to envision it.

—Author unknown

I've learned that the person with big dreams is more powerful than the one with all the facts.

—H. Jackson Brown, Jr.

If we want new and better schools, we must become new and better people.

—Marilyn Ferguson

Excellence is not a destination, but a journey.

—Author unknown

Changing a curriculum is like moving a cemetery—until you try it, you will never realize how many friends the dead have.

—Author unknown

You can't make change if you don't have any coins.

—Al Logsdon

You must change values, then beliefs, then behavior.

—Clinton Bunke

The real voyage of discovery consists not in seeking a new landscape, but in seeing with new eyes.

—Marcel Proust

We must be willing to change what we do in our classrooms so students can grow—not hope that students can grow so we don't have to change what we do in our classrooms.

—Todd Whitaker

One doesn't discover new lands without con-
senting to lose sight of the shore for a very
long time.

—Andre Gide

A ship in port is safe, but that's not what
ships are built for.

—Grace Hopper

Never doubt that a small group of thought-
ful, committed people can change the world;
indeed, it is the only thing that has.

—Margaret Mead

When someone says it can't be done, it only
means they can't do it.

—Author unknown

There are three kinds of people in this world: those who make things happen, those who watch things happen, and those who wonder what's happening.

—Author unknown

Don't be so busy looking for problems that you forget to notice the improvement.

—Todd Whitaker

Wrong is wrong even if everyone does it. Right is right even if no one does it.

—Author unknown

If the fish keep getting sick, change the water.

—Gary Phillips

Enthusiasm is everything. It must be taut and vibrating like a guitar string.

—Pelé

Our children can begin to experience fulfillment as soon as we choose to create environments permitting them to do so.

—Bob Samples

Diversity is the one true thing we all have in common—celebrate it today.

—Author unknown

Some minds are like finished concrete—thoroughly mixed and permanently set.

—Author unknown

Great Quotes for Great Educators

Those people who talk about when they would like to retire probably already have.

—Marv Levy

People who say they are burned out probably were never on fire in the first place.

—Author unknown

In order to do the work that must be done, we must stop the work we are doing.

—Matthew Fox

I hated every minute of training, but I said, "Don't quit. Suffer now and live the rest of your life as a champion."

—Muhammad Ali

There is only one corner of the universe you can be certain of improving, and that's your own self.

—Aldous Huxley

The more frequently a person acts like a fool, the greater the odds that it is not an act.

—Todd Whitaker

Failure is not fatal, but failure to change might be.

—John Wooden

Even if you're on the right track, you'll get run over if you just sit there.

—Will Rogers

Great Quotes for Great Educators

To be an innovator, you can't be worried about making mistakes.

—Julius Erving

If you want truly to understand something, try to change it.

—Kurt Lewin

The only difference between a rut and a grave is the depth of the hole.

—Roland Barth

You never get ahead of anyone as long as you're trying to get even with him.

—Lou Holtz

The rung of a ladder was never meant to rest upon, but only to hold a man's foot long enough to enable him to put the other somewhat higher.

—Thomas Huxley

It is not enough to understand what we ought to be, unless we know what we are. And we don't understand what we are unless we know what we ought to be.

—T. S. Eliot

Obstacles are those frightful things you see when you take your eyes off your goal.

—Henry Ford

You see things and say, "Why?", but I dream things that never were and say, "Why not?"

—George Bernard Shaw

If you don't dream, you may as well be dead.

—George Foreman

The only person who loves a change is a wet baby.

—Ray Blitzer

Whether teachers who teach the way they did 20 years ago are a problem depends mostly on how they taught 20 years ago.

—Todd Whitaker

Change is inevitable; growth is optional.

—Author unknown

The Winds of Change

The dogmas of the quiet past are inade-quate to the stormy present.

—Abraham Lincoln

Success is how high you bounce when you hit bottom.

—George S. Patton

The tragedy of life doesn't lie in not reach-ing your goal. The tragedy lies in having no goal to reach.

—Benjamin E. Mays

I'm not comfortable being preachy, but more people need to start spending as much time in the library as they do on the basket-ball court.

—Kareem Abdul-Jabbar

Human beings, who are almost unique in having the ability to learn from the experience of others, are also remarkable for their apparent disinclination to do so.

—Douglas Adams

Champions aren't made in gyms. Champions are made from something they have deep inside them—a desire, a dream, a vision.

—Muhammad Ali

It is much easier to stand next to a heavyset person than it is to stick to a diet.

—Todd Whitaker

Freedom is not worth having if it does not include the freedom to make mistakes.

—Mahatma Gandhi

I keep six honest serving men
(They taught me all I knew):
Their names are What and Why and When
And How and Where and Who.

—Rudyard Kipling

For a better life, eat breakfast every day,
drink plenty of water, get plenty of sleep,
and laugh.

—Dale Lumpa

Always be in a state of becoming.

—Walt Disney

Most of us would rather hold on to a familiar
pain than trade it for an unfamiliar plea-
sure.

—Author unknown

We are not going to solve today's problems relying on the past's paradigm.

—Author Unknown

Echoes

Real Quotes from Real Students

- *My sixth-grade teachers always believed in me, even when I messed up.*

- *My ninth-grade teacher asked how she could help me, not what was my problem when I was having a hard time at home.*

- *My tenth-grade history teacher opened a new world to me. He helped inflame a passion in me towards the environment and world traveling/exploring.*

- *I just finished my research paper and used the information in a political conversation!*

- *I like preschool because I know more tonight than I knew yesternight.*

Teamwork— Together We Can Do It All

11

> We try to see some good in everybody we meet, but sometimes we have to squint.
>
> Todd Whitaker

Nothing is impossible for the man who doesn't have to do it himself.

—A. H. Weiler

If students do not see their teachers work successfully together, they may never see two adults work successfully together.

—Todd Whitaker

The greatest mistake is to create an environment in which people are afraid to work because they are afraid to make a mistake.

—B. Alcorn

Individual commitment to a group effort—that is what makes a team work, a company work, a society work, and a civilization work.

—Vince Lombardi

We cannot change alone.

—Gary Phillips

We are there for the students, not the other way around.

—Todd Whitaker

Don't take yourself too seriously, but know when to be serious.

—Author unknown

It takes two to speak the truth—one to speak, the other to hear.

—Henry David Thoreau

All too often we are giving young people cut flowers when we should be teaching them to grow their own plants.

—John W. Gardner

Students need choices and voices.

—Author unknown

I don't think we can win every game- just the next one.

—Lou Holtz

If you want to lose your students quickly, brag about yourself. If you want to build relationships with your students, brag about them.

—Todd Whitaker

A system is a perceived whole whose elements "hang together" because they continually affect each other over time and operate toward a common purpose.

—Peter Senge

Rich is not how much you have, or where you are going, or even what you are. Rich is who you have beside you.

—Jack I. Kohler II

A hole in the boat is a hole in the whole boat.

—Author unknown

Take blame and give credit.

—Dale Lumpa

I've learned that enthusiasm and success just seem to go together.

—Felix Abisheganaden

A man may make mistakes, but he isn't a failure until he starts blaming someone else.

—John Wooden

Art is I; science is we.

—Claude Bernard

Compete against yourself, not others, for that is who is truly your best competition.

—Peggy Fleming

If two people agree on everything, then we don't need two people.

—Todd Whitaker

Do not underestimate the importance of helping people recognize what they already know.

—Michael Quinn Patten

Together Everyone Achieves More.

—Author unknown

Teamwork is the fuel that allows common people to attain uncommon results.

—Andrew Carnegie

Success demands singleness of purpose.

—Vince Lombardi

Nothing will work unless you do.

—Maya Angelou

If you are going to expect a student to read between the lines, it is helpful if you write big.

—Todd Whitaker

R + R - R = R + R
(<u>R</u>ules and <u>R</u>egulations minus <u>R</u>elationships equals <u>R</u>esentment and <u>R</u>ebellion)

—Author unknown

The most important measure of how good a game I played was how much better I made my teammates play.

—Bill Russell

Coming together is a beginning; keeping together is progress; working together is success.

—Henry Ford

One student working with you is worth twenty-five students working for you.

—Todd Whitaker

If it has been done, it can be done.

—Ron Edmonds

If a teacher is gone, we call a sub. If a principal is gone, we don't even bother. But if the secretary is gone, we might as well close the school!

—*Todd Whitaker*

Echoes

Real Quotes from Real Students

- *I remember my principal knowing my name and helping me unlock my bike.*

- *My favorite teacher helps me when I do not understand and also eats with us every day.*

- *My favorite memory was making the plays in high school and realizing that you are always your worst critic, but only those outside the circle can be your judge.*

- *My favorite teacher does things with us, not to us.*

- *I learned the most today when my teacher sat by me on the floor.*

If you would like information about inviting Todd Whitaker to speak to your group, please contact him at t-whitaker@indstate.edu or at his web site www.toddwhitaker.com or (812) 237-2904.

If you would like information about inviting Dale Lumpa to speak to your group, please contact him at dalelumpa@aol.com or call (303) 715-9319.

What Great Teachers Do Differently:
Fourteen Things That Matter Most
Todd Whitaker

*This book is a quick read and is packed with good stuff.
It is filled with humor that makes the book readable, in-
teresting and "real."*
> —Barbara McPherson, Principal
> Stony Point North Elementary School
> Kansas City, KS

What Great Teachers Do Differently describes the beliefs, behaviors, attitudes, and interactions that form the
fabric of life in our best classrooms and schools. It focuses
on the specific things that great teachers do...that others
do not. It answers these essential questions:

- Is it high expectations for students that matter?

- How do great teachers respond when students
  misbehave?

- Do great teachers filter differently than their
  peers?

- How do the best teachers approach standardized testing?

2004, 144 pp. paperback 1-930556-69-1
$29.95 plus shipping and handling

Order form on page 199

Motivating and Inspiring Teachers:
The Educational Leader's Guide
for Building Staff Morale
Todd Whitaker, Beth Whitaker, and Dale Lumpa

"The most appealing feature of this book is its simplicity and common sense. It is practical, useful and readable, and I recommend it."

—Ron Seckler, Principal
Swope Middle School, NV

Filled with strategies to motivate and stimulate your staff, this book features simple suggestions that you can integrate into your current daily routines. It will show you how to:

♦ insert key phrases and specific actions into your day-to-day conversations, staff meetings, and written memos to stimulate peak effectiveness

♦ hire new staff and plan orientation and induction meetings to cultivate and retain loyal and motivated staff members

♦ use the "gift of time" to stimulate and reward

♦ get amazing results by not taking credit for them

♦ motivate yourself each and every day

2000, 252 pp. paperback 1-883001-99-4
$34.95 plus shipping and handling

Order form on page 199

What Great Principals Do Differently:
15 Things That Matter Most
Todd Whitaker

"... affirming and uplifting, with insights into human nature and 'real people' examples..."
—Edward Harris, Principal
Chetek High School, WI

What are the specific qualities and practices of great principals that elevate them above the rest? Blending school-centered studies and experience working with hundreds of administrators, Todd Whitaker reveals why these practices are effective and demonstrates how to implement each of them in your school.

Brief Contents

♦ It's People, Not Programs

♦ Who is the Variable?

♦ Hire Great Teachers

♦ Standardized Testing

♦ Focus on Behavior, Then Focus on Beliefs

♦ Base Every Decision on Your Best Teachers

♦ Make it Cool to Care

♦ Set Expectations At the Start of the Year

♦ Clarifying Your Core

2003, 130 pp. paperback 1-930556-47-0
$29.95 plus shipping and handling

Order form on page 199

Dealing with Difficult Teachers
Second Edition
Todd Whitaker

"... filled with inspirational ideas and strategies that work."

—Melanie Brock, Principal
Westview Elementary School
Excelsior Springs, MO

Whether you are a teacher, administrator, or fill some other role in your school, difficult teachers can make your life miserable. This book shows you how to handle staff members who:

- gossip in the teacher's lounge.
- consistently say "it won't work" when any new idea is suggested.
- undermine your efforts toward school improvement.
- negatively influence other staff members.

Added to this edition are 4 new chapters on communicating with difficult teachers.

This new section demonstrates how to:

- eliminate negative behaviors.
- implement effective questioning strategies.
- apply the "The Best Teacher/Worst Teacher" test.

2002, 208 pp. paperback 1-930556-45-4
$29.95 plus shipping and handling

Order form on page 199

Teaching Matters:

Motivating & Inspiring Yourself
Todd and Beth Whitaker

"This book makes you want to be the best teacher you can be."
> —Nancy Fahnstock, Godby High School
> Tallahassee, Florida

Celebrate the teaching life! This book helps teachers:

♦ rekindle the excitement of the first day of school all year long

♦ approach every day in a "Thank God it is Monday" frame of mind

♦ not let negative people ruin your day

♦ fall in love with teaching all over again

Brief Contents

♦ Why You're Worth it

♦ Unexpected Happiness

♦ Could I Have a Refill Please? (Opportunities for Renewal)

♦ Celebrating Yourself

♦ Raise the Praise–Minimize the Criticize

♦ Making School Work for You

2002, 150 pp. paperback 1-930556-35-7
$24.95 plus shipping and handling

Order form on page 199

Dealing with Difficult Parents
(And with Parents in Difficult Situations)
Todd Whitaker and Douglas J. Fiore

"This book is an easy read with common sense appeal. The authors are not afraid to share their own vulnerability and often demonstrate a sense of humor."
—Gale Hulme, Program Director
Georgia's Leadership Institute
for School Improvement

This book helps teachers, principals, and other educators develop skills in working with the most difficult parents in the most challenging situations. It shows you how to:

- avoid the "trigger" words that serve only to make bad situations worse.

- use the right words and phrases to help you develop more positive relationships with parents.

- deal with parents who accuse you of not being fair.

- build positive relationships with even the most challenging parents.

2001, 175 pp. paperback 1-930556-09-8
$29.95 plus shipping and handling

Order form on page 199

Six Types of Teachers:
Recruiting, Retaining, and Mentoring the Best
Douglas J. Fiore and Todd Whitaker

"The examples of the six types of teachers were awesome. This book is a valuable resource for principals and all others who hire and retain teachers."
—Jeff Remelius, Assistant Principal
Rogers Middle School, MO

This book helps you sharpen your ability to

- hire better teachers for your school,
- improve the ones who are already there, and
- keep your best and brightest on board.

It demonstrates that the quality of the people on your staff will ultimately determine the quality of your school—and the success of your students.

Six Types of Teachers: Recruiting, Retaining and Mentoring the Best is organized around a framework to help you identify quality teachers. Among the six types of teachers revealed are the WOWs (the ones who walk on water), the Solids (dependable, hardworking contributors to the good of the school), the ones who are "not bad" but Replaceable...and three *other* types of teachers.

2005, 170 pp. (est.) paperback. 1-930556-85-3
$29.95 plus shipping and handling

Order form on page 199

Feeling Great!
The Educator's Guide for Eating Better, Exercising Smarter, and Feeling Your Best
Todd Whitaker and Jason Winkle

"This book will especially appeal to people who do not like to exercise."

—Katherine Alvestad
Dowell Elementary School, MD

Educators spend so much time taking care of others that we sometimes forget to take care of ourselves! This book will help teachers, principals, professors, and all educators find time in our busy schedules to focus on our physical self. You will learn how to:

♦ make time for exercise in your hectic daily schedule.

♦ learn how to feel your best every day.

♦ eat right even when on the go.

♦ keep your fitness momentum going all year.

♦ turn your daily routines into healthy habits.

Brief Contents

♦ Why Fitness for Educators? What's So Special About Us?

♦ But I Don't Like to Sweat

♦ Setting Realistic Goals

♦ Finding the Time and the Energy

♦ Keeping it up Through the Summer

♦ Fad or Fact? What Diets Really Work?

2002, 150 pp. paperback 1-930556-38-1
$24.95 plus shipping and handling

Order form on page 199

ORDER FORM

☐ **Great Quotes for Great Teachers.** Whitaker and Lumpa. 2005. 208 pp. paperback 1-930556-82-9. $29.95 plus shipping and handling.

☐ **What Great Teachers Do** *Differently*: **14 Things That Matter Most.** Whitaker. 2003. 130 pp. paperback 1-930556-69-1. $29.95 plus shipping and handling.

☐ **Motivating and Inspiring Teachers: The Educator's Guide for Building Staff Morale.** Whitaker, Whitaker, and Lumpa. 2000. 252 pp. paperback 1-883001-99-4. $34.95 plus shipping and handling.

☐ **What Great Principals Do** *Differently*: **15 Things That Matter Most.** Whitaker. 2002. 130 pp. paperback 1-930556-47-0. $29.95 plus shipping and handling.

☐ **Dealing with Difficult Teachers**, Second Edition. Whitaker. 2002. 208 pp. paperback 1-930556-45-4. $29.95 plus shipping and handling.

☐ **Teaching Matters: Motivating & Inspiring Yourself.** Whitaker and Whitaker. 2002. 150 pp. paperback. 1-930556-35-7. $24.95 plus shipping and handling.

☐ **Dealing with Difficult Parents (And with Parents in Difficult Situations).** Whitaker and Fiore. 2001. 175 pp. paperback 1-930556-09-8. $29.95 plus shipping and handling.

☐ **Six Types of Teachers: Recruiting, Retaining, and Mentoring the Best.** 2005. 176 pp. pagerback 1-930556-85-3. $29.95 plus shipping and handling.

☐ **Feeling Great! The Educator's Guide for Eating Better, Exercising Smarter, and Feeling Your Best.** Whitaker and Winkle. 2002. 150 pp. paperback 1-930556-38-1. $24.95 plus shipping and handling.

Fill in your address on other side

Please place your check and/or purchase order with this form in an envelope and mail to *Eye On Education*. If you are not satisfied with any book, simply return it within 30 days in saleable condition for full credit or refund.

Ship to: _____
          Name

_____
School

_____
Address

_____
City   State   Zip

_____
Phone   Your title

Bill to: _____
          Name

_____
School

_____
Address

_____
City   State   Zip

_____
Phone   Your title

Subtotal (books)   _____

Shipping and Handling   _____

Total   _____

Shipping and Handling:

1 Book—Add $6.00   2 Books—Add $10.00   3 Books—Add $13.00
4 Books—Add $15.00   5–7 Books—Add $17.00 8–11 Books—Add $19.00

Method of Payment (choose one):

☐ Check (enclosed)   ☐ Credit Card   ☐ Purchase Order

_____   _____
Credit card # (Visa, Master Card, Discover) or PO #   Expiration Date

6 Depot Way West
Larchmont, N.Y. 10538
(914) 833–0551 Phone (914) 833–0761 Fax
www.eyeoneducation.com